THE SCIENCE OF STRESS RELIEF

Tackle Daily Stress Effectively, Improve Focus and Productivity, Master Relaxation Techniques Easily, and Achieve a Lifetime of Stress-Free Living

Freddy Joy

ABOUT THE AUTHOR

Freddy Joy, Author of "The Science of Stress Relief."

Freddy Joy never set out to become a writer. Her journey began with a simple yet profound desire—to share her experiences and insights on managing stress and boosting productivity to lead a fulfilling life. Armed with a strong academic foundation, she holds a Master's degree in Psychology (MSc) from Dr. B.R. Ambedkar Open University, specializing in practical applications of research in human behavior and psychology. Additionally, she earned a "Certificate in Community Health" from Indira Gandhi National Open University, equipping her with knowledge to address key issues in public health.

Freddy lives in Guntur, Andhra Pradesh, India, where she balances her professional pursuits with her most cherished role as a mother of two. Whenever she can, she devotes her time to her children, finding joy and inspiration in their presence. Her writing is a testament to her passion for helping others navigate life's challenges and unlock their true potential.

CONTENTS

Breaking Free from Stress — VII

1. Understanding Stress - The Root Cause of Overwhelm — 1

2. The Mind-Body Connection - Tapping Into Inner Calm — 10

3. Practical Stress Management - Tools for Daily Life — 18

4. Mastering Focus and Productivity Under Pressure — 27

5. The Art of Relaxation - Transforming Stress into Serenity — 35

6. Long-Term Solutions for a Stress-Free Life — 43

Conclusion: A New Chapter of Calm and Control — 51

References and Resources 55

Disclaimer 63

BREAKING FREE FROM STRESS

"It's not stress that kills us; it is our reaction to it." – Hans Selye

Introduction: The Weight We Carry

In today's fast-paced world, stress is no longer an occasional inconvenience—it's a chronic companion for many. From the constant ping of notifications to the demands of balancing work and personal life, stress levels are at an all-time high. According to the American Psychological Association, over 77% of adults regularly experience physical symptoms caused by stress, such as headaches and fatigue, while 73% report experiencing psychological symptoms like anxiety.

Stress isn't just a mental issue; it's a full-body phenomenon. Left unchecked, it contributes to chronic illnesses, weakens the immune system, and disrupts mental clarity. More alarmingly, stress has infiltrated every aspect of modern living, from the boardroom to the dining table.

This chapter unpacks the science of stress, exploring its physiological and psychological effects. It also provides actionable solutions, backed by research, to help you take control of your stress and reclaim your peace of mind.

Key Insights: The Science of Stress and How to Tackle It

1. The Modern Epidemic of Stress

Stress has evolved from being an evolutionary response to danger—think fight or flight—to becoming a daily occurrence. Today, instead of lions, our threats include deadlines, emails, and endless to-do lists.

Scientific Insight: Chronic stress triggers the release of cortisol, the body's primary stress hormone. Elevated cortisol levels over time can lead to severe health issues, including cardiovascular disease, diabetes, and even memory impairment. A 2019 study published in *Nature Communications* revealed that individuals with persistently high cortisol levels had significantly smaller brain volumes in areas responsible for memory and emotional regulation.

Real-Life Story: Meet Sarah, a marketing executive in her mid-thirties. Sarah's career soared, but her stress levels skyrocketed too. Sleepless nights, chronic headaches, and a short temper became her norm. It wasn't until a fainting episode during a critical presentation that she realized her stress was controlling her life. Sarah's journey toward stress relief began with a simple breathing exercise app, leading her to meditation and healthier boundaries at work. Today, Sarah not only manages her stress but uses her story to inspire her team.

2. Why Stress Relief Matters Now More Than Ever

Stress doesn't just steal your peace—it hijacks your productivity, relationships, and overall well-being. Left unaddressed, chronic stress contributes to burnout, a condition recognized by the World Health Organization as a significant workplace hazard.

Emerging Trends:

- **Digital Minimalism**: Constant connectivity amplifies stress. Adopting practices like turning off notifications or scheduling tech-free hours can drastically reduce mental clutter.

- **Stress Management for Remote Workers**: With blurred boundaries between work and home, strategies like creating dedicated workspaces and adhering to strict work hours are proving essential.

Real-Life Story: John, a freelance graphic designer, faced the challenges of working from home during the pandemic. Without clear boundaries, his work hours stretched into his evenings, leaving him perpetually exhausted. By adopting stress management tools like the Pomodoro technique and setting tech-free evenings, John turned his chaotic routine into one of balance and productivity.

3. The Science Behind Stress: What Happens in Your Body and Mind

Stress activates the autonomic nervous system, leading to physiological changes like increased heart rate, rapid breathing, and heightened alertness. While short bursts of stress can boost performance—known as eustress—chronic stress wreaks havoc.

Key Research:

- A study from Harvard Medical School highlights that mindfulness practices can reduce cortisol levels by up to 25%.

- Research from Stanford University's Stress Management Lab shows that regular exercise decreases stress perception by altering neural responses to stress triggers.

Actionable Tips:

- **Mindfulness Practices**: Incorporate 10 minutes of meditation into your daily routine. Apps like Calm or Headspace can be great starting points.

- **Exercise for Stress Relief**: Aim for 30 minutes of moderate exercise daily. Activities like walking, yoga, or swimming are particularly effective.

4. How This Book Will Help You Take Control

The good news? Stress is manageable with the right tools and mindset. This book isn't just a guide—it's your roadmap to understanding and overcoming stress. You'll learn:

- The science behind stress and how to use it to your advantage.

- Practical techniques to reduce stress in real-time.

- Long-term strategies to prevent stress from taking over your life.

Interactive Element: Throughout this book, you'll find habit trackers and stress-relief templates to help you apply these techniques in your daily life. These tools are designed to make stress management actionable and sustainable.

Conclusion: A New Perspective on Stress

Stress is inevitable, but suffering is optional. By understanding the science of stress and adopting evidence-based strategies, you can transform stress from a source of chaos into a catalyst for growth.

Actionable Takeaways:

1. Identify your primary stressors by journaling for five minutes daily.

2. Incorporate one stress-relief technique—like deep breathing or a 10-minute walk—into your daily routine.

3. Set clear boundaries, such as no work emails after 7 PM, to create a healthier work-life balance.

Remember, managing stress is not about eliminating it entirely but learning to navigate it effectively. With the strategies in this book, you're equipped to handle whatever comes your way.

Resources for Further Reading

1. *Why Zebras Don't Get Ulcers* by Robert M. Sapolsky

2. *The Upside of Stress* by Kelly McGonigal

3. "Mindfulness-Based Stress Reduction (MBSR)" research by Jon Kabat-Zinn

4. "Stress Management and Resilience Training" study by Mayo Clinic

5. *Digital Minimalism* by Cal Newport

6. Harvard Medical School: "The Science of Mindfulness"

7. American Psychological Association: "Stress Effects on the Body"

8. *Atomic Habits* by James Clear (Chapter on habit stacking for stress relief)

9. Research on cortisol and stress: *Nature Communications*, 2019

10. Stanford's Stress Management Lab: "The Role of Exercise in Stress Management"

Chapter 1

UNDERSTANDING STRESS – THE ROOT CAUSE OF OVERWHELM

"You cannot always control what goes on outside. But you can always control what goes on inside." – Wayne Dyer

What Is Stress? The Good, the Bad, and the Ugly

Stress is often painted as the villain of modern life, but it's not inherently bad. In its simplest form, stress is the body's response to any demand or challenge. This response, known as the "fight or flight" mechanism, evolved to protect us from threats, such as a predator in the wild.

The Good: Stress can be a motivator. Known as *eustress*, this positive form of stress pushes us to meet deadlines, ace presentations, or train for a marathon. A 2016 study in the *Journal of Personality and Social Psychology* found that moderate levels of stress can enhance performance and resilience.

The Bad: Problems arise when stress becomes chronic. Repeated exposure to stressors without adequate recovery leads to burnout, anxiety, and physical health issues. Chronic stress is linked to cardiovascular disease, gastrointestinal problems, and weakened immunity, as highlighted in research from the American Institute of Stress.

The Ugly: When stress is unmanaged, it can spiral into a debilitating state. This leads to *distress*, a harmful level of stress that disrupts daily functioning, relationships, and overall well-being.

How Stress Impacts Your Brain and Body

When stress hits, the brain triggers a cascade of hormonal changes. The hypothalamus signals the adrenal glands to release adrenaline and cortisol, leading to increased heart rate, rapid breathing, and heightened alertness. While these responses are helpful in short bursts, prolonged activation can wreak havoc on the body.

Key Effects on the Brain:

- **Memory Impairment**: Chronic stress shrinks the hippocampus, the part of the brain responsible for memory and learning. A 2018 study in *Nature Reviews Neuroscience* found that high cortisol levels over time impair memory retrieval and learning ability.

- **Emotional Regulation**: Stress disrupts the prefrontal cortex, impairing decision-making and increasing emotional reactivity.

Key Effects on the Body:

- **Heart Health**: Elevated stress increases blood pressure and the risk of heart disease.

- **Digestive Issues**: Stress reduces blood flow to the digestive system, causing nausea, bloating, or chronic conditions like IBS.

Real-Life Story: Maria, a 45-year-old teacher, noticed her memory slipping and her patience wearing thin during her school's transition to online learning. Her doctor diagnosed her with chronic stress after noticing elevated cortisol levels. Through cognitive behavioral therapy (CBT) and mindfulness techniques, Maria regained control over her stress, demonstrating how recovery is possible with proactive steps.

The Hidden Triggers: Recognizing Your Personal Stressors

Stress isn't one-size-fits-all; it's highly personal. Identifying your triggers is the first step toward managing them.

Common Triggers:

1. **Workplace Stress**: Deadlines, office politics, and unrealistic expectations.

2. **Financial Worries**: Debt, bills, or lack of savings.

3. **Relationships**: Conflicts or lack of support from loved ones.

4. **Health Concerns**: Chronic illness or fear of the unknown.

5. **Lifestyle Factors**: Poor sleep, lack of exercise, and

unhealthy diets.

Emerging Triggers:

- **Information Overload**: The 24/7 news cycle and social media updates.

- **Fear of Missing Out (FOMO)**: Constant comparison via social media amplifies stress and dissatisfaction.

Actionable Step: Keep a "stress journal" for a week, noting when you feel stressed, what triggered it, and how you responded. Patterns will emerge, helping you pinpoint and address your unique stressors.

Stress in the Digital Age: Breaking the Cycle of Overstimulation

The digital age, while offering convenience, has become a double-edged sword. Constant notifications, endless scrolling, and the pressure to always be connected fuel a state of overstimulation.

Scientific Insight:

- A study in the *Journal of Behavioral Addictions* found that excessive smartphone use increases anxiety and reduces sleep quality.

- Digital multitasking has been shown to decrease cognitive efficiency and increase stress levels, as noted in a 2019 report from Stanford University.

Breaking Free:

1. **Turn Off Notifications**: Designate specific times to check your phone instead of reacting to every ping.

2. **Schedule Tech-Free Hours**: Set aside one hour daily for activities without screens—reading, exercising, or meditating.

3. **Use Apps Mindfully**: Leverage apps like Freedom or Forest to limit distractions and encourage focus.

4. **Create a Digital Detox Plan**: Once a month, unplug entirely for a day to reset your mind and body.

Real-Life Story: Kevin, a software engineer, felt overwhelmed by the constant barrage of Slack messages, emails, and social media updates. After implementing a "digital sunset" rule—shutting off screens an hour before bed—he experienced better sleep, reduced anxiety, and greater clarity in his work.

Conclusion: Understanding Is the First Step to Relief

Stress is complex, but understanding its causes, effects, and triggers is the foundation for managing it effectively. Recognizing that stress is not the enemy—but an indicator of imbalance—empowers you to take control. By identifying your unique stressors and leveraging tools like journaling and digital minimalism, you can break free from the cycle of overwhelm.

Actionable Takeaways:

1. Identify your top three stress triggers this week and brainstorm solutions for each.

2. Start a stress journal to track patterns and adjust your responses.

3. Implement one digital detox habit, like tech-free meals or no screens an hour before bed.

By taking small, consistent steps, you can reduce the impact of stress and lay the groundwork for a calmer, healthier life.

CHAPTER 2

THE MIND-BODY CONNECTION - TAPPING INTO INNER CALM

"Calm mind brings inner strength and self-confidence, so that's very important for good health." – Dalai Lama

The Power of Breath: Simple Techniques to Relax Instantly

The simplest and most accessible tool to manage stress lies right under your nose—your breath. Conscious breathing is a cornerstone of stress management, allowing you to calm your nervous system and reset your mind within moments.

Why Breath Matters:Breathing directly influences the autonomic nervous system. Deep, controlled breaths activate the parasympathetic nervous system, which slows your heart rate and promotes relaxation.

Scientific Insight:A 2017 study published in *Frontiers in Psychology* found that slow, deep breathing significantly reduces cortisol levels and improves heart rate variability, a key marker of resilience to stress.

Techniques to Try:

1. **Box Breathing**: Inhale for four counts, hold for four counts, exhale for four counts, and pause for four counts. Repeat this cycle four times.

2. **4-7-8 Breathing**: Inhale through the nose for four counts, hold for seven counts, and exhale slowly for eight counts. This method is particularly effective for calming anxiety and promoting sleep.

3. **Diaphragmatic Breathing**: Place one hand on your chest and the other on your belly. Breathe deeply into your belly, ensuring the hand on your chest stays still.

Real-Life Story: Sarah, a busy ER nurse, used box breathing during chaotic shifts. Within weeks, she reported feeling more in control of her emotions and less overwhelmed, even during high-pressure situations.

Mindful Awareness: How to Stay Present and Reduce Anxiety

Mindfulness, the practice of staying fully present in the moment, is a powerful antidote to stress and anxiety. By focusing on the present, you can break free from the mental spirals of worry about the past or future.

How Mindfulness Works:Mindfulness engages the prefrontal cortex, the brain region responsible for decision-making and emotional regulation. This reduces activity in the amygdala, the brain's fear center, creating a sense of calm and control.

Practical Mindfulness Practices:

1. **The 5-4-3-2-1 Technique**: To ground yourself during moments of anxiety, identify five things you see, four things you feel, three things you hear, two things you smell, and one thing you taste.

2. **Mindful Eating**: Pay attention to the colors, textures, and flavors of your food to create a moment of calm during meals.

3. **Body Scan Meditation**: Lie down, close your eyes, and bring awareness to each part of your body, starting at your toes and moving upward.

Scientific Support:A study in *JAMA Internal Medicine* (2014) demonstrated that an eight-week mindfulness program significantly reduced anxiety and improved sleep quality in participants.

Real-Life Story: Mark, a tech startup founder, started incorporating mindfulness into his daily routine using a simple app. He found himself less reactive during high-stakes meetings, improving both his decision-making and his relationships with colleagues.

Rewiring Your Brain with Neuroplasticity for Stress Relief

Your brain has the incredible ability to rewire itself—a phenomenon known as neuroplasticity. This means that with consistent practice, you can train your brain to respond to stress more effectively.

How Neuroplasticity Works:Neuroplasticity involves creating and strengthening neural pathways. Repeatedly practicing calming behaviors—like mindfulness or breathing exercises—forms new pathways in the brain that make these responses habitual over time.

Evidence from Neuroscience:Dr. Sara Lazar's research at Harvard University found that mindfulness meditation thickens the prefrontal cortex and hippocampus, areas associated with emotional regulation and memory.

Building Stress-Resilient Habits:

1. **Gratitude Journaling**: Spend five minutes daily writing down three things you're grateful for. Gratitude strengthens positive neural pathways, reducing stress and improving mood.

2. **Visualization**: Visualize yourself remaining calm and in control during a stressful situation. This primes your brain to adopt the behavior in real life.

3. **Reframing Thoughts**: Practice identifying and reframing negative thoughts into neutral or positive ones to shift your perspective on stressful events.

Harnessing Your Body's Natural Relaxation Response

The relaxation response is your body's built-in mechanism to counteract stress. Discovered by Dr. Herbert Benson of Harvard Medical School, this state is the physiological opposite of the fight-or-flight response.

How to Activate It:

1. **Progressive Muscle Relaxation (PMR)**: Tense each muscle group for 5 seconds, then release. Start from your toes and work your way up.

2. **Meditation**: Even five minutes of focused breathing or guided meditation can lower stress levels.

3. **Yoga**: Combining physical movement with mindful breathing, yoga is an excellent way to engage the relaxation response.

Scientific Validation: Dr. Benson's research showed that the relaxation response reduces blood pressure, heart rate, and stress hormones. A 2019 meta-analysis in *Psychosomatic Medicine* further confirmed that relaxation techniques significantly improve mental health and physiological markers of stress.

Real-Life Story: Lisa, a mother of two and small business owner, practiced PMR every evening for a month. She reported better sleep, improved patience with her children, and a more optimistic outlook on her busy life.

Conclusion: Aligning Mind and Body for Inner Calm

Understanding and harnessing the mind-body connection is key to managing stress effectively. Through simple yet powerful techniques like conscious breathing, mindfulness, and activating the relaxation response, you can create lasting calm in your daily life.

Actionable Takeaways:

1. Start each day with a two-minute breathing exercise to set a calm tone.

2. Practice mindfulness during mundane tasks, like washing dishes or walking, to train your focus.

3. Try one relaxation technique, such as PMR or yoga, for 10 minutes before bed.

With practice, these habits will not only reduce stress but also create a more resilient and harmonious mind-body connection, empowering you to face life's challenges with clarity and ease.

CHAPTER 3

PRACTICAL STRESS MANAGEMENT - TOOLS FOR DAILY LIFE

"It's not stress that kills us; it is our reaction to it." – Hans Selye

Time Management Hacks to Reduce Stress

Stress often stems from feeling overwhelmed by a lack of time. Effective time management can transform chaos into control, allowing you to approach tasks with clarity and purpose.

Why Time Management Matters:
When you manage your time well, you reduce

procrastination, prioritize effectively, and create mental space for relaxation. This minimizes the mental clutter that contributes to stress.

Proven Strategies:

1. **The Eisenhower Matrix**: Categorize tasks into four quadrants—urgent and important, not urgent but important, urgent but not important, and neither urgent nor important. Focus on the first two categories and delegate or eliminate the rest.

2. **Time Blocking**: Allocate specific time slots for focused work, meetings, and breaks. Research from *The Journal of Applied Psychology* suggests that structured time blocking can increase productivity and decrease stress.

3. **The Two-Minute Rule**: If a task takes less than two minutes, do it immediately. This reduces the buildup of minor tasks that can weigh on your mind.

Real-Life Story: Alex, a software engineer juggling tight deadlines, adopted the Eisenhower Matrix and time-blocking techniques. Within weeks, he found himself less frazzled and more productive, freeing up evenings for family time.

Decluttering Your Life: Simplify to Find Peace

A cluttered environment often mirrors a cluttered mind. Simplifying your physical and mental space can have profound stress-relieving benefits.

The Science of Decluttering:
A study published in *Personality and Social Psychology Bulletin* found that individuals with cluttered homes had higher cortisol levels than those with organized spaces.

Steps to Simplify:

1. **Start Small**: Begin with one area, like your desk or closet, and set a timer for 15 minutes. Decluttering in short bursts prevents overwhelm.

2. **Adopt the One-In-One-Out Rule**: For every new item you bring into your space, remove an old one.

3. **Digital Decluttering**: Organize your email inbox, unsubscribe from unnecessary newsletters, and streamline your apps.

Mental Decluttering:

- Write down your worries to free up mental bandwidth.

- Use mindfulness techniques to focus on the present rather than ruminating on past or future stressors.

Real-Life Story: Mia, a freelance writer, decluttered her workspace and adopted a minimalist approach to her possessions. The process not only reduced her stress but also improved her creativity and focus.

Healthy Habits for Stress-Free Living: Sleep, Nutrition, and Exercise

Your lifestyle choices significantly impact how your body and mind respond to stress. By prioritizing foundational habits like sleep, proper nutrition, and regular exercise, you can build resilience to stress.

The Role of Sleep:
Sleep is when your body repairs itself and processes emotions. Chronic sleep deprivation increases cortisol levels and impairs decision-making.

- **Actionable Tip**: Maintain a consistent sleep schedule, even on weekends. Avoid screens an hour before bed to support melatonin production.

The Power of Nutrition:
What you eat fuels your brain and body. Nutrient deficiencies can exacerbate stress, while a balanced diet supports emotional stability.

- **Superfoods for Stress**: Incorporate magnesium-rich foods like spinach, omega-3s from fish or flaxseeds, and antioxidant-rich berries to combat oxidative stress.

Exercise as Stress Relief:

Physical activity releases endorphins, which act as natural stress relievers. Regular exercise also lowers cortisol levels over time.

- **Actionable Tip**: Even a 20-minute brisk walk can reduce stress and improve mood. Choose an activity you enjoy to make it sustainable.

Scientific Backing:

A 2018 review in *The Lancet Psychiatry* found that individuals who exercised regularly had 43% fewer days of poor mental health compared to non-exercisers.

Real-Life Story: Raj, a financial analyst, struggled with stress-induced insomnia. By adopting a routine of morning walks and adding magnesium-rich foods to his diet, he experienced better sleep and a calmer mindset within a month.

Setting Boundaries and Saying No Without Guilt

A significant source of stress is overcommitting and failing to set clear boundaries. Learning to say "no" without guilt is a powerful skill for protecting your time and energy.

Why Boundaries Matter:
Boundaries define what is acceptable in your life. Without them, others may unknowingly overstep, leading to burnout and resentment.

How to Set Healthy Boundaries:

1. **Be Clear and Firm**: State your boundaries in a respectful yet assertive manner. For example, "I can't take on this project right now, but I'd be happy to help next month."

2. **Practice Saying No**: Start with small, low-stakes situations to build confidence.

3. **Use "I" Statements**: Focus on your needs rather than accusing the other person. For instance, "I need some quiet time to recharge after work."

Letting Go of Guilt:
Remind yourself that saying no allows you to say yes to things that truly matter. It's an act of self-respect, not selfishness.

Scientific Insight:
Research published in *Psychological Science* highlights that

people who prioritize their well-being by setting boundaries report lower stress levels and greater life satisfaction.

Real-Life Story: Laura, a small business owner, struggled with saying no to her clients. By practicing boundary-setting and using assertive communication, she reduced her workload, improved her health, and strengthened her client relationships.

Conclusion: Building a Toolbox for Stress-Free Living

Practical stress management is about equipping yourself with tools and habits that empower you to navigate daily challenges with ease. By mastering time management, decluttering your life, prioritizing healthy habits, and setting boundaries, you can create a balanced and fulfilling lifestyle.

Actionable Takeaways:

1. Implement the Eisenhower Matrix for better task prioritization.

2. Declutter one small area of your home or digital space today.

3. Incorporate at least one superfood into your diet and commit to 20 minutes of daily physical activity.

4. Practice saying "no" in a low-stakes situation to protect your energy.

With these strategies, you'll not only manage stress but also create a foundation for lasting peace and productivity.

CHAPTER 4

MASTERING FOCUS AND PRODUCTIVITY UNDER PRESSURE

"You cannot always control circumstances, but you can control your focus." – Tony Robbins

Overcoming Procrastination and Mental Blocks

The Procrastination Trap:

Procrastination is often a stress response, triggered by fear of failure, perfectionism, or feeling overwhelmed. Overcoming it requires a mindset shift and actionable strategies.

Root Causes of Procrastination:

1. Fear of imperfection.

2. Lack of clarity or direction.

3. Overestimating the effort needed to complete tasks.

Science-Backed Techniques to Beat Procrastination:

- **The 5-Minute Rule**: Commit to working on a task for just five minutes. This often breaks inertia and motivates you to continue.

- **Chunking**: Divide large tasks into smaller, manageable steps to reduce overwhelm.

- **Reward Systems**: Tie task completion to a small reward, leveraging dopamine to reinforce positive behavior.

Real-Life Example: Sarah, a graduate student, constantly delayed writing her thesis. By breaking her work into daily 500-word goals and rewarding herself with her favorite coffee after each session, she completed her thesis weeks ahead of the deadline.

Building Resilience in High-Stress Situations

Resilience as a Skill:

Resilience isn't about avoiding stress but learning to adapt and thrive despite it. Cultivating this skill allows you to maintain focus and productivity even in challenging circumstances.

Steps to Build Resilience:

1. **Reframe Challenges**: Shift your mindset to view obstacles as opportunities for growth.

2. **Create a Support Network**: Connect with mentors, peers, or friends who can offer guidance and encouragement.

3. **Practice Gratitude**: Focus on what's going well to counteract the negative impact of stress.

Scientific Insight:

A study published in *Frontiers in Psychology* found that individuals who practiced gratitude journaling experienced a significant reduction in stress and an increase in problem-solving abilities.

Real-Life Example: James, a startup founder, navigated a critical funding crisis by reframing the situation as an opportunity to rethink his business strategy. His resilience not only secured new funding but also strengthened his team's confidence in his leadership.

The Flow State: How to Achieve Deep Focus Effortlessly

What Is Flow?

Flow is a state of deep focus and immersion where tasks feel almost effortless. Coined by psychologist Mihaly Csikszentmihalyi, flow is linked to peak productivity and creativity.

Elements of Flow:

1. **Clear Goals**: Knowing exactly what you want to achieve helps focus your attention.

2. **Immediate Feedback**: Quick responses to your actions keep you engaged.

3. **Balanced Challenge**: Tasks should be challenging enough to be engaging but not so difficult that they cause frustration.

How to Enter Flow:

- **Eliminate Distractions**: Silence notifications, declutter your workspace, and set boundaries to protect your focus time.

- **Warm-Up Rituals**: Engage in a short routine, like deep breathing or journaling, to signal your brain it's time to work.

- **Work in Sprints**: Use techniques like the Pomodoro Technique (25 minutes of work followed by a 5-minute break) to maintain energy and focus.

Scientific Backing:

Neuroscience research shows that during flow, the brain produces higher levels of dopamine, norepinephrine, and anandamide, enhancing focus and mood.

Real-Life Example: Emily, a graphic designer, used morning rituals and distraction-free work sessions to achieve flow while designing her most complex project yet, earning praise from her clients.

Leveraging Breaks and Micro-Relaxation for Peak Productivity

The Importance of Breaks:

Contrary to popular belief, working without breaks can

diminish productivity and increase stress. Short, intentional breaks refresh your mind and help maintain sustained focus.

Effective Break Strategies:

1. **The 90-Minute Work Cycle**: Research by sleep scientist Nathaniel Kleitman suggests working in 90-minute cycles, followed by a 15-minute break, aligns with your body's natural ultradian rhythms.

2. **Micro-Relaxation**: Take brief pauses to perform calming activities like stretching, deep breathing, or mindfulness exercises.

3. **Nature Breaks**: A walk outdoors can significantly reduce stress and improve creative problem-solving.

Scientific Insight:
A study published in *Cognition* found that short breaks during tasks improved participants' accuracy and performance by 16%.

Real-Life Example: Rajiv, a corporate lawyer, adopted the 90-minute work cycle and used his breaks for yoga stretches. This routine enhanced his focus and lowered his stress during long, intense workdays.

Conclusion: Thriving Under Pressure

Mastering focus and productivity under pressure isn't about avoiding stress altogether—it's about developing strategies that help you manage it effectively. By overcoming procrastination, building resilience, entering flow states, and using breaks strategically, you can turn pressure into an opportunity for growth.

Actionable Takeaways:

1. Apply the 5-Minute Rule to overcome procrastination.

2. Start a gratitude journal to build resilience.

3. Use the Pomodoro Technique or 90-minute work cycles to maintain focus.

4. Incorporate micro-relaxation techniques like deep breathing or nature walks into your day.

With these tools, you can thrive even in high-pressure situations, achieving not just productivity but also a sense of fulfillment and balance.

CHAPTER 5

THE ART OF RELAXATION - TRANSFORMING STRESS INTO SERENITY

"Almost everything will work again if you unplug it for a few minutes, including you."
– Anne Lamott

Guided Relaxation Techniques for Instant Calm

The Science of Relaxation: Guided relaxation activates the parasympathetic nervous system, reducing heart rate and calming the mind. Techniques like progressive muscle relaxation and body scans are effective for immediate stress relief.

Techniques to Try:

1. **Progressive Muscle Relaxation (PMR)**: Focus on tensing and releasing muscles group by group, starting from your toes and moving upward.

2. **Body Scans**: Mentally "scan" your body for tension, and consciously release it.

3. **Breath-Focused Meditation**: Close your eyes, take slow, deep breaths, and count each inhale and exhale.

Scientific Support:

Research published in *Psychosomatic Medicine* shows that PMR significantly reduces cortisol levels and improves sleep quality.

Real-Life Example: Maria, an emergency nurse, used guided body scans during her lunch breaks to transition from high stress to calm, enabling her to perform better during long shifts.

Visualization and Positive Affirmations to Reset Your Mind

Harnessing the Mind's Power:

Visualization and affirmations tap into your brain's ability to reframe stress, fostering a sense of control and optimism.

Steps for Visualization:

1. Close your eyes and picture a peaceful, happy place—like a beach or a forest.

2. Imagine yourself calm and in control, successfully navigating your current stressor.

Crafting Effective Affirmations:

1. Keep them positive: "I am capable of handling this."

2. State them in the present tense: "I am calm and resilient."

3. Repeat daily for reinforcement.

Scientific Insight:
Studies in *The Journal of Behavioral Medicine* reveal that visualization reduces anxiety by activating the same neural pathways as experiencing calm in real life.

Real-Life Example: After a corporate downsizing, Steve used affirmations like "I am prepared for new opportunities" while visualizing himself succeeding in job interviews. This practice helped him stay confident and land a better position.

The Role of Creativity and Hobbies in Stress Relief

Why Creativity Matters:
Engaging in creative hobbies like painting, writing, or gardening can act as a therapeutic outlet, reducing stress by fostering mindfulness and joy.

Benefits of Hobbies:

- **Flow State**: Creativity often induces a flow state, a powerful antidote to stress.

- **Sense of Accomplishment**: Completing a creative project boosts self-esteem.

- **Distraction from Worries**: Focusing on a hobby redirects attention away from stressors.

Scientific Backing:
A study in *Art Therapy* found that 45 minutes of creative activity significantly lowered stress-related hormones in participants.

Real-Life Example: Lisa, a high school teacher, took up watercolor painting during the pandemic. This creative outlet became her sanctuary, helping her stay balanced while navigating remote teaching challenges.

Nature's Healing Power: Reconnecting with the Outdoors

The Science of Nature Therapy:
Spending time outdoors is proven to reduce stress, lower

proven to reduce stress, lower blood pressure, and boost mood. Activities like walking, hiking, or simply sitting in a park can restore mental clarity.

Benefits of Green Spaces:

1. **Reduced Cortisol Levels**: Nature immersion lowers stress hormones.

2. **Improved Focus**: Natural environments enhance cognitive function and attention.

3. **Increased Happiness**: Sunlight triggers serotonin production, lifting mood.

Ideas to Reconnect with Nature:

- Morning walks in a local park.

- Weekend hikes in nearby trails.

- Gardening or maintaining indoor plants for a touch of greenery.

Scientific Insight:
A 2019 study in *Frontiers in Psychology* found that spending

just 20 minutes in nature significantly reduced cortisol levels in urban dwellers.

Real-Life Example: Raj, a software engineer, struggled with burnout until he began taking daily 15-minute walks in his neighborhood park. This simple habit transformed his energy and mental clarity.

Conclusion: Serenity Is Within Your Reach

Relaxation isn't a luxury—it's a skill that can be cultivated with the right techniques. Guided relaxation, visualization, creativity, and nature are powerful tools to transform stress into serenity.

Actionable Takeaways:

1. Practice progressive muscle relaxation or body scans for immediate calm.

2. Create a daily affirmation to reinforce a positive mindset.

3. Dedicate time to a creative hobby that brings you joy.

4. Commit to spending at least 20 minutes in nature

every day.

By incorporating these strategies into your life, you can master the art of relaxation and build a foundation of calm that empowers you to navigate stress with grace and confidence.

LONG-TERM SOLUTIONS FOR A STRESS-FREE LIFE

"It is not stress that kills us; it is our reaction to it." – Hans Selye

Cultivating Gratitude and Positivity for Emotional Well-Being

The Science of Gratitude:

Gratitude shifts your focus from what's wrong to what's right, fostering emotional resilience. Regular gratitude practices enhance well-being by rewiring the brain to focus on positivity.

Simple Gratitude Practices:

1. **Gratitude Journaling**: Write three things you're thankful for each day.

2. **Expressing Appreciation**: Tell someone why you value them, strengthening your relationships.

3. **Mindful Reflection**: Pause to acknowledge small joys, like a sunny day or a good meal.

Scientific Evidence:

Research in *The Journal of Positive Psychology* shows that people who write weekly gratitude lists report higher levels of happiness and lower levels of stress.

Real-Life Story: After recovering from a serious illness, Megan began a daily gratitude journal to combat lingering anxiety. Over time, she noticed a marked improvement in her outlook and ability to manage stress.

Building a Supportive Social Network

Why Connections Matter:

Social relationships act as a buffer against stress, offering emotional support, practical help, and a sense of belonging.

Strategies to Strengthen Your Network:

1. **Quality Over Quantity**: Prioritize a few deep, meaningful relationships over many superficial ones.

2. **Be Vulnerable**: Sharing your challenges fosters trust and deeper connections.

3. **Give and Receive Support**: Offer help to others and accept help when needed.

Scientific Insight:
Studies in *Health Psychology* reveal that people with strong social networks are less likely to experience stress-related illnesses.

Real-Life Story: David, a busy entrepreneur, joined a local support group for small business owners. Sharing his struggles and hearing others' stories helped him feel less isolated and more equipped to handle stress.

The Role of Professional Help: When to Seek Therapy or Counseling

Understanding When to Seek Help:
While many stressors can be managed independently, chronic stress, anxiety, or depression may require professional intervention. Therapy offers tools to understand and address stress more effectively.

Signs You May Need Support:

- Persistent feelings of overwhelm or hopelessness.

- Physical symptoms like insomnia or fatigue that don't improve.

- Difficulty functioning at work or in relationships.

Types of Therapy for Stress Management:

1. **Cognitive Behavioral Therapy (CBT)**: Helps reframe negative thought patterns.

2. **Mindfulness-Based Stress Reduction (MBSR)**: Combines meditation and body awareness.

3. **Solution-Focused Therapy**: Concentrates on practical steps to overcome challenges.

Scientific Support:

A review in *JAMA Psychiatry* highlights that CBT is highly effective in reducing stress and anxiety symptoms.

Real-Life Story: After years of high-pressure deadlines, Priya sought counseling to address chronic stress. Through CBT, she learned techniques to manage her workload and emotions effectively, regaining her balance.

Developing a Personal Stress Management Plan for Lifelong Success

Why a Plan Matters:
Stress management is not a one-size-fits-all approach. A personalized plan ensures that strategies align with your unique needs and lifestyle.

Steps to Create Your Plan:

1. **Identify Triggers**: Keep a stress journal to track patterns.

2. **Choose Techniques That Work for You**: Experiment with relaxation methods, exercise, or hobbies.

3. **Set Realistic Goals**: Start small, such as meditating for 5 minutes a day, and build gradually.

4. **Review and Adjust Regularly**: Periodically assess your plan and refine it as needed.

Interactive Tools:
Use habit trackers or apps like Calm or Headspace to maintain consistency.

Scientific Evidence:

The *American Psychological Association* emphasizes that structured stress management plans improve coping skills and reduce the impact of stress over time.

Real-Life Story: Emily, a college student, created a stress management plan that included yoga, journaling, and a strict no-screen time policy before bed. Her tailored approach helped her excel academically while maintaining mental clarity.

Conclusion: A Lifetime of Balance and Peace

Long-term stress relief requires consistent effort, but the rewards are profound. By cultivating gratitude, building a supportive network, seeking professional help when necessary, and developing a personalized stress management plan, you can create a foundation for lifelong serenity.

Actionable Takeaways:

1. Start a gratitude journal to shift your mindset daily.

2. Strengthen your social connections by nurturing meaningful relationships.

3. Consider therapy if stress feels unmanageable or overwhelming.

4. Develop a tailored stress management plan that evolves with your needs.

By integrating these practices into your life, you're not just managing stress—you're creating a life defined by balance, resilience, and joy.

CONCLUSION: A NEW CHAPTER OF CALM AND CONTROL

"You cannot always control what goes on outside. But you can always control what goes on inside." – Wayne Dyer

Reflecting on Your Journey Toward Stress Relief

As you reach the end of this journey, it's worth taking a moment to reflect on how far you've come. Understanding the science behind stress, mastering relaxation techniques, and building sustainable habits have empowered you with tools to face challenges with clarity and confidence.

Take pride in the progress you've made. Recognizing small victories along the way reinforces your commitment to maintaining a stress-free lifestyle.

Daily Practices to Sustain Your New Lifestyle

Sustaining the benefits of stress relief requires consistency. Here are simple practices to integrate into your daily routine:

1. **Morning Rituals**: Start your day with mindful breathing or journaling to set a positive tone.

2. **Midday Resets**: Incorporate brief moments of mindfulness during your workday to stay grounded.

3. **Evening Wind-Down**: Dedicate time to relaxation techniques like guided meditation before bed.

By anchoring these practices to your schedule, they become effortless habits that keep stress at bay.

Embracing Challenges as Opportunities for Growth

Stressful situations are inevitable, but your perspective makes all the difference. Viewing challenges as opportunities to learn and grow transforms adversity into a stepping stone for personal development.

When faced with stress:

- **Pause and Assess**: Take a moment to evaluate the situation objectively.

- **Apply Your Tools**: Use the techniques you've learned, such as mindful awareness or visualization.

- **Celebrate Your Resilience**: Acknowledge your ability to adapt and thrive despite difficulties.

Your Path Forward: Living a Life Free from Stress

As you continue on your path, remember that the goal is not to eliminate stress entirely but to manage it effectively. Life's unpredictability can be a source of excitement and growth when approached with the right mindset and tools.

Key Takeaways for Your Stress-Free Journey:

- Regularly revisit the practices and strategies you've learned.

- Build a supportive network to share your challenges and triumphs.

- Seek joy in the simple moments of life.

- Keep evolving your personal stress management plan to align with new circumstances.

By staying committed to these principles, you open a new chapter of calm, control, and fulfillment. This is your opportunity to live a life not just free from stress but full of purpose, peace, and joy.

A Final Thought:

The power to live a stress-free life lies in your hands. Armed with the knowledge and tools you've gained, you're ready to face life's challenges with resilience, grace, and unwavering calm. Your journey has just begun—step forward with confidence.

REFERENCES AND RESOURCES

B elow is a curated list of references and resources to support the content of the chapters in *The Science of Stress Relief*. These materials include scientific studies, books, and tools that readers can explore for further learning.

General Resources

1. **Books:**

   - *Why Zebras Don't Get Ulcers* by Robert Sapolsky

   - *The Relaxation Response* by Herbert Benson

   - *The Power of Now* by Eckhart Tolle

   - *Atomic Habits* by James Clear

- *Mindfulness for Beginners* by Jon Kabat-Zinn

2. Scientific Studies:

- American Psychological Association (APA): Stress in America Reports

- National Institute of Mental Health (NIMH): Coping with Stress

3. Apps and Tools:

- Calm (meditation and sleep support)

- Headspace (mindfulness and meditation app)

- Todoist (for time management)

Chapter 1: Understanding Stress—The Root Cause of Overwhelm

1. Books:

- *The Stress Effect* by Henry L. Thompson

- *Burnout: The Secret to Unlocking the Stress Cycle* by Emily Nagoski and Amelia Nagoski

2. **Scientific Studies**:

- McEwen, B. S. (1998). *Stress, adaptation, and disease. Allostasis and allostatic load. Annals of the New York Academy of Sciences.*

- Cohen, S., et al. (1995). *Psychological stress and susceptibility to the common cold. The New England Journal of Medicine.*

Chapter 2: The Mind-Body Connection—Tapping Into Inner Calm

1. **Books**:

- *The Body Keeps the Score* by Bessel van der Kolk

- *Breath: The New Science of a Lost Art* by James Nestor

2. **Scientific Studies**:

- Lazar, S. W., et al. (2005). *Meditation experience is associated with increased cortical thickness. NeuroReport.*

- Benson, H., et al. (1974). *The relaxation response.*

Psychiatry.

3. **Tools**:

- Insight Timer (meditation app with guided breathing exercises)

Chapter 3: Practical Stress Management—Tools for Daily Life

1. **Books**:

- *Essentialism: The Disciplined Pursuit of Less* by Greg McKeown

- *The Life-Changing Magic of Tidying Up* by Marie Kondo

2. **Scientific Studies**:

- Baer, R. A. (2003). *Mindfulness training as a clinical intervention: A conceptual and empirical review. Clinical Psychology: Science and Practice.*

- Owens, J. A. (2014). *Sleep loss and its consequences for health, performance, and safety. Medical Clinics of North America.*

3. **Tools**:

- MyFitnessPal (to track nutrition and exercise)

- Sleep Cycle (app for optimizing sleep patterns)

Chapter 4: Mastering Focus and Productivity Under Pressure

1. **Books**:

- *Deep Work: Rules for Focused Success in a Distracted World* by Cal Newport

- *The Willpower Instinct* by Kelly McGonigal

2. **Scientific Studies**:

- Csikszentmihalyi, M. (1990). *Flow: The psychology of optimal experience.*

- Steel, P. (2007). *The nature of procrastination: A meta-analytic and theoretical review of quintessential self-regulatory failure. Psychological Bulletin.*

3. **Tools**:

- Focus@Will (music for productivity)

- Pomodoro Tracker (for managing focus intervals)

Chapter 5: The Art of Relaxation—Transforming Stress into Serenity

1. **Books**:

- *Visualization for Beginners* by Cassandra Sturdy

- *Big Magic: Creative Living Beyond Fear* by Elizabeth Gilbert

2. **Scientific Studies**:

- Kabat-Zinn, J. (1982). *An outpatient program in behavioral medicine for chronic pain patients based on the practice of mindfulness meditation: Theoretical considerations and preliminary results. General Hospital Psychiatry.*

- Kaplan, S. (1995). *The restorative benefits of nature: Toward an integrative framework. Journal of Environmental Psychology.*

3. **Tools**:

- Nature Sounds App (for relaxation and focus)

- Art Supplies for creative stress relief activities

Chapter 6: Long-Term Solutions for a Stress-Free Life

1. **Books**:

   - *The Gifts of Imperfection* by Brené Brown

   - *Thanks! How Practicing Gratitude Can Make You Happier* by Robert Emmons

2. **Scientific Studies**:

   - Fredrickson, B. L. (2001). *The role of positive emotions in positive psychology: The broaden-and-build theory of positive emotions. American Psychologist.*

   - Holt-Lunstad, J., et al. (2010). *Social relationships and mortality risk: A meta-analytic review. PLoS Medicine.*

3. **Resources**:

- American Counseling Association (www.counseling.org)

- BetterHelp (online therapy platform)

These resources provide a robust foundation for deeper understanding and practical application of stress relief strategies covered in *The Science of Stress Relief.*

DISCLAIMER

This book is for educational purposes only. Readers acknowledge that the author does not render legal, financial, medical, or professional advice. The content within this book has been derived from various sources. Please consult a licensed professional before attempting any techniques outlined in this book.

By reading this document, the reader agrees that under no circumstances is the author responsible for any direct or indirect losses incurred as a result of the use of the information contained within this document, including but not limited to errors, omissions, or inaccuracies.

Adherence to all applicable laws and regulations, including international, federal, state, and local governing professional licensing, business practices, advertising, and all other jurisdictions, is the sole responsibility of the purchaser or reader.

Neither the author nor the publisher assumes any responsibility or liability whatsoever on behalf of the purchaser or reader of these materials. Any perceived slight of any individual or organization is purely unintentional.